Cinematogi

Job Hunting
A Practical Manual for Job-Hunters and Career-Changers

Write a review to receive any *FREE* eBook from our Catalogue - $99 Value!

If you recently bought this book we would love to hear from you! Benefit from receiving a free eBook from our catalogue at http://www.emereo.org/ if you write a review on Amazon (or the online store where you purchased this book) about your last purchase!

How does it work?

To post a review on Amazon, just log in to your account and click on the Create your own review button (under Customer Reviews) of the relevant product page. You can find examples of product reviews in Amazon. If you purchased from another online store, simply follow their procedures.

What happens when I submit my review?

Once you have submitted your review, send us an email at review@emereo.org with the link to your review, and the eBook you would like as our thank you from http://www.emereo.org/. Pick any book you like from the catalogue, up to $99 RRP. You will receive an email with your eBook as download link. It is that simple!

**Good solid advice and great strategies
for getting interviews and landing the Cinematographers job.**

To Prepare for the Job this book tells you:

- the training and education needed
- earnings
- expected job prospects
- the job's activities and responsibilities
- working conditions

To Land the Job, it gives you the hands-on and how-to's insight on

- Finding Opportunities - the best places to find them
- Writing Unbeatable Resumes and Cover Letters
- Acing the Interview
- What to Expect From Recruiters
- How employers hunt for Job-hunters.... and More

This book offers excellent, insightful advice for everyone from entry-level to senior professionals. None of the other such career guides compare with this one. It stands out because it:

1. Explains how the people doing the hiring think, so that you can win them over on paper and then in your interview;
2. Is filled with useful cheat and work-sheets;
3. Explains every step of the job-hunting process - from little-known ways for finding openings to getting ahead on the job.

This book covers everything. Whether you are trying to get your first Job or move up in the system, you will be glad you got this book.

Contents

Cinematographers

Summary, What Cinematographers do, Work Environment, How to become a Cinematographers, Pay, Job Outlook, Similar Occupations, Contacts for More Information

FINDING AND APPLYING FOR Cinematographers JOBS AND EVALUATING OFFERS

Where to Learn About Job Openings; Job Search Methods; Personal contacts. ; School career planning and placement offices. ; Employers. ; Classified ads. ; Internet resources. ; Labor unions. ; State employment service offices. ; Job matching and referral. ; Services for special groups. ; Federal Government. ; Community agencies. ; Private employment agencies and career consultants. ; Internships.

Applying for a Cinematographers Job

Resumes and application forms. ; Gathering information. ; Choosing a format. ; Resume and KSA (knowledge, skills & abilities) tips:; Cover letters.

Cinematographers Job Interview Tips

Preparation:; Personal appearance:; The interview:; Information to bring to an interview:

Evaluating a Cinematographers Job Offer

The organization. ; Should you work for a relatively new organization or one that is well established?

The job

Where is the job located?; Does the work match your interests and make good use of your skills?; How important is the job to the company or organization?; What will the hours be?; How long do most people who enter this job stay with the company?; The company should have a training plan for you. ; Salaries and benefits.

WHAT TO EXPECT FROM THE OTHER SIDE OF THE TABLE...

THE INTERVIEW AND SELECTION PROCESS; Step 1 ; Technical Competencies Assessment Guide; Step 2; Determine the Customer Service Focused ; Competencies of the Job; Definitions:; Responsible. ; Likeable. ; Believable. ; Outgoing. ; Unflappable. ; CUSTOMER SERVICE FOCUSED BEHAVIORS ASSESSMENT GUIDE; Step 3 ; Develop Interview Questions to Assess Both ; Technical and Customer Service ; Focused Competencies; Step 4; Conducting the Interview; Step 5; Background and Reference Checks; Making a Job Offer; Confirming Job Offer Letter; Informing Unsuccessful Candidates; Retention of Interview Materials

SAMPLE CUSTOMER SERVICE FOCUSED INTERVIEW QUESTIONS

Responsible; Likeable; Believable; Outgoing; Unflappable

INTERVIEWING Cinematographers

A Practical Guide for Selecting

THE INTERVIEW PROCESS

Planning; Confirming/Scheduling Interview; Conducting the Interview; Closing; Follow Up

TIPS ON INTERVIEWING Cinematographers

Interview Questions To Get You Started; Supervisor and Manager Competencies; Interviewing People With Disabilities; Accommodating Persons With Disabilities For An Interview; Interview Do's and Don'ts

CHECKING REFERENCES

Which References Should I Check?; Tips for Checking References; The Reference Check Questions To Ask; Prohibited Questions and Practices

RECORDING A PROFILE OF IMPRESSIONS

Supervisory and Managerial Competencies:; Building Coalitions/Communication:

Recruiting Cinematographers - It Takes More Than A Job Announcement

Before Submitting the Vacancy; When the Vacancy Announcement is Open; Once the Certificate of Eligibles is Received; After The Selection is Made

ASSESSING YOUR RECRUITMENT AND SELECTION PRACTICES

Policies and Procedures; Recruitment Strategies

GLOSSARY

"There are few, if any, jobs in which ability alone is sufficient. Needed, also, are loyalty, sincerity, enthusiasm and team play." - William B. Given, Jr.

"When people go to work, they shouldn't have to leave their hearts at home." - Betty Bender

"One machine can do the work of fifty ordinary men. No machine can do the work of one extraordinary man." - Elbert Hubbard

"To find joy in work is to discover the fountain of youth." - Pearl S. Buck

"One of the symptoms of an approaching nervous breakdown is the belief that one's work is terribly important." - Bertrand Russell

"Opportunity is missed by most people because it is dressed in overalls and looks like work." - Thomas A. Edison

"Far and away the best prize that life offers is the chance to work hard at work worth doing." - Theodore Roosevelt

"Going to work for a large company is like getting on a train. Are you going sixty miles an hour or is the train going sixty miles an hour and you're just sitting still?" - J. Paul Getty

"The world is full of willing people, some willing to work, the rest willing to let them." - Robert Frost

"So much of what we call management consists in making it difficult for people to work." - Peter Drucker

"Nothing is really work unless you would rather be doing something else." - James M. Barrie

"I'm a great believer in luck, and I find the harder I work the more I have of it." - Thomas Jefferson

"Success in business requires training and discipline and hard work. But if you're not frightened by these things, the opportunities are just as great today as they ever were." - David Rockefeller

Cinematographers FACTS:

Summary, What Cinematographers do, Work Environment, How to become one, Pay, Job Outlook, Similar Occupations and Contacts for More Information.

Film and Video Editors and Camera Operators

Summary

Editors and camera operators sometimes work on location.

Quick Facts: Film and Video Editors and Camera Operators

2010 Median Pay $45,490 per year

$21.87 per hour

Entry-Level EducationBachelor's degree

Work Experience in a Related Occupation   See How to Become One

On-the-job Training   See How to Become One

Number of Jobs, 2010   58,300

Job Outlook, 2010-20 4% (Slower than average)

Employment Change, 2010-20   2,200

What Film and Video Editors and Camera Operators Do

Film and video editors and camera operators record images that entertain or inform an audience. Camera operators capture a wide range of material for TV shows, motion pictures, music videos, documentaries, or news and sporting events. Editors construct the final productions from the many different images camera operators capture. They collaborate with producers and directors to create the final production.

Work Environment

Most camera operators work in the motion picture industry or television broadcasting. Editors are employed largely by the motion picture industry, although some work in broadcasting.

How to Become a Film and Video Editor or Camera Operator

Camera operators typically need a bachelor's degree and some on-the-job training. Most film editors have a bachelor's degree and several years of experience as an assistant to a film editor.

Pay

The median annual wage of camera operators was $40,390 in May 2010. The median annual wage of film and video editors was $50,930 in May 2010.

Job Outlook

Employment of film and video editors and camera operators is projected to grow 4 percent from 2010 to 2020, slower than the average for all occupations. These occupations should have intense competition for jobs, and those with more experience at a TV station or on a film set will likely have the best job prospects.

Similar Occupations

Compare the job duties, education, job growth, and pay of film and video editors and camera operators with similar occupations.

O*NET

O*NET provides comprehensive information on key characteristics of workers and occupations.

Contacts for More Information

Learn more about film and video editors and camera operators by contacting these additional resources.

What Film and Video Editors and Camera Operators Do

Most video editing is done digitally.

Film and video editors and camera operators record images that entertain or inform an audience. Camera operators capture a wide range of material for TV shows, motion pictures, music videos, documentaries, or news and sporting events. Editors construct the final productions from the many different images that camera operators capture. They collaborate with producers and directors to create the final production.

Duties

Camera operators and film and video editors typically do the following:

Choose and present interesting material for an audience

Work with a director to determine the overall vision of the production

Discuss filming and editing techniques with a director to improve a scene

Select the appropriate equipment, from type of camera to software for editing

Shoot or edit a scene based on the director's vision

Most camera operators have one or more assistants working under their supervision. The assistants set up the camera equipment and may be responsible for storing it and caring for it. They also help the operator determine the best shooting angle and make sure that the camera stays in focus.

Likewise, editors usually have a few assistants. The assistant supports the editor by keeping track of each shot in a database. Assistants may do some editing themselves.

The increased use of digital filming has changed the work of many camera operators and editors. Many camera operators prefer using digital cameras, because these instruments give the operator more angles to shoot from. Digital cameras have also changed the job of some camera assistants: instead of loading film or choosing lenses, they download digital images or choose a type of software program to use with the camera.

Nearly all editing work is done on a computer, and editors often are trained in a specific type of editing software.

The following are examples of types of camera operators.

Studio camera operators work in a broadcast studio and videotape their subjects from a fixed position. There may be one or several cameras in use at a time. Operators normally follow directions that give the order of the shots. They often have time to practice camera movements before shooting begins. If they are shooting a live event, they must be able to make adjustments at a moment's notice and follow the instructions of the show's director.

Electronic news gathering (ENG) operators work on location as part of a reporting team. ENG operators follow events as they unfold and often record live events or breaking news. To capture these events, operators must anticipate the action and act quickly to shoot it. They sometimes edit their own footage in the field and then send it back to a studio to be broadcast.

Cinematographers film motion pictures. They usually have a team of camera operators and assistants working under them. They determine the best angles and types of cameras to capture a shot.

They may use stationary cameras that shoot whatever passes in front of them or use a camera mounted on a track and move around the action. Some operators sit on cranes and follow the action. Others carry the camera on their shoulder while they move around the action.

Some cinematographers specialize in filming cartoons or special effects.

Videographers film or videotape private ceremonies or special events, such as weddings. They also may work with companies and make corporate documentaries on a variety of topics. Some videographers post short videos on websites for businesses. Most videographers edit their own material.

Many videographers run their own business or do freelance work. They may submit bids, write contracts, and get permission to shoot on locations that may not be open to the public. They also get copyright protection for their work and keep financial records.

Work Environment

Camera operators shoot a wide range of images.

Camera operators held about 26,800 jobs in 2010. About 24 percent work in television broadcasting and another 21 percent work in motion picture and video industries. About 34 percent of camera operators are self-employed.

Film and video editors held about 31,600 jobs in 2010. About 42 percent are employed by motion picture and video industries and 9 percent work in television broadcasting. About 35 percent of editors are self-employed.

Electronic news gathering (ENG) operators usually travel locally and may have to stay overnight to cover a major event. Cinematographers and operators who film movies or TV shows may film on location and be away from home for months at a time. Operators who travel usually carry heavy equipment.

Some camera operators work in uncomfortable or even dangerous conditions, such as severe weather, military conflicts, and natural disasters. They may have to stand for long periods waiting for an event to take place. They may carry heavy equipment.

Work Schedules

Work hours vary with the type of operator or editor, though most work full time. Those who work in broadcasting might have to work long hours to meet a deadline. Those who work in the motion picture industry may have long, irregular hours while filming but go through a period of unemployment after their work on the film is complete and before they are hired for their next job.

How to Become a Film and Video Editor or Camera Operator

Camera operators are usually responsible for reloading their camera.

Camera operators typically need a bachelor's degree and some on-the-job training. Most film editors have a bachelor's degree and several years of experience as an assistant to a film editor.

Education

Most camera operator and editor positions require a bachelor's degree in a field related to film or broadcasting. Many colleges offer courses in camera operation or video editing software.

Camera operators must have an understanding of digital cameras and computer technology, because both are now used on film sets. Most editing is now done digitally, so film and video editors should have experience with different types of video editing software. Most editors eventually specialize in one type of software, but beginners should be familiar with as many as possible.

Training

On movie sets, many camera operators start out as a production assistant for the camera department to learn how film production works. Production assistants typically run errands or do simple tasks for operators. With some moderate on-the-job training production assistants can become camera assistants and, eventually, operators.

In broadcasting, operators also begin as an assistant and work their way up to operator. Operators typically start out working for a small TV station or on a small movie set. As they become more experienced, they move on to larger productions.

Work Experience

Most film editors have had several years of experience in related jobs before they are given an opportunity as an editor. They normally start out as an edit room assistant, taking notes or doing other simple tasks for an editor, before becoming an assistant editor. After several years of learning about editing as an assistant, they may be given an opportunity as an editor.

Like camera operators, editors typically start out on small productions and move on to bigger and more expensive ones as they gain experience.

Advancement

Some camera operators or editors become producers or directors. For more information, see the profile on producers and directors.

Important Qualities

Creativity. Camera operators and editors should be able to imagine what the result of their filming or editing will look like to an audience.

Detail oriented. Editors look at every frame of film and decide what should be kept and what should be cut to make the best production.

Hand–eye coordination. In the field, camera operators need to be able to move about the action while holding a camera steady.

Technical skills. Camera operators must understand the high-end cameras they use. Editors must know how to use many features of sophisticated editing software.

Visual skills. Camera operators must be able to see clearly what they are filming.

Pay

Film and Video Editors and Camera Operators

Median annual wages, May 2010

Film and Video Editors

$50,930

Film and Video Editors and Camera Operators

$45,490

Camera Operators, Television, Video, and Motion Picture

$40,390

Total, All Occupations

$33,840

All Occupations includes all occupations in the U.S. Economy.

The median annual wage of camera operators was $40,390 in May 2010. The median wage is the wage at which half the workers in an occupation earned more than that amount and half earned less. The lowest 10 percent earned less than $20,300, and the top 10 percent earned more than $81,270.

The median annual wage of film and video editors was $50,930 in May 2010. The lowest 10 percent earned less than $25,960, and the top 10 percent earned more than $111,860.

Work hours vary with the type of operator or editor, though most work full time. Those who work in broadcasting might have to work long hours to meet a deadline. Those who work in the motion picture industry may have long, irregular hours while filming but endure a period of unemployment after their work on the film is complete and before they are hired for their next job.

Job Outlook

Film and Video Editors and Camera Operators

Percent change in employment, projected 2010-20

Total, All Occupations

14%

Film and Video Editors

5%

Film and Video Editors and Camera Operators

4%

Camera Operators, Television, Video, and Motion Picture

2%

All Occupations includes all occupations in the U.S. Economy.

Employment of camera operators is projected to experience little or no change, growing 2 percent from 2010 to 2020.

In broadcasting, job growth is expected to be slow because automatic camera systems reduce the need for camera operators at many TV stations. Despite the public's continued strong demand for new movies and TV shows, companies won't hire as many people as might be expected as the motion picture industry becomes more productive. They will be able to produce more movies without hiring many more workers.

Production companies are experimenting with new content delivery methods, such as mobile and online TV, which may lead to more work for operators in the future. However, these delivery methods are still in their early stages, and it remains to be seen how successful they will be.

Employment of film and video editors is projected to grow 5 percent from 2010 to 2020, slower than the average for all occupations.

In broadcasting, the consolidation of roles, such as field reporters who edit their own work, may lead to fewer of jobs for editors at TV stations. However, more editors are expected to be needed in the motion picture industry because of an increase in special effects, which are complicated and require more planning.

Job Prospects

There will be some job openings due to workers leaving the occupation, however, camera operators and film and video editors will still face strong competition for jobs. The broadcasting and motion picture industries attract many more applicants than there are jobs available. Those with more experience at a TV station or on a film set should have the best job prospects.

Employment projections data for film and video editors and camera operators, 2010-20

Occupational Title	SOC Code	Employment, 2010	Projected Employment, 2020	Change, 2010-20	Employment by Industry
				Percent	Numeric

Television, Video, and Motion Picture Camera Operators and Editors

| 27-4030 | 58,300 | 60,500 | 4 | 2,200 |

Camera Operators, Television, Video, and Motion Picture

27-4031   26,800 27,300 2   600

Film and Video Editors

27-4032   31,600 33,200 5   1,600

Similar Occupations

This table shows a list of occupations with job duties that are similar to those of film and video editors and camera operators.

OCCUPATIONJOB DUTIES ENTRY-LEVEL EDUCATION MEDIAN ANNUAL PAY, MAY 2010

Actors

Actors express ideas and portray characters in theater, film, television, and other performing arts media. They also work at theme parks or for other live events. They interpret a writer's script to entertain or inform an audience.

Some college, no degree   The annual wage is not available.

Broadcast and Sound Engineering Technicians

Broadcast and sound engineering technicians set up, operate, and maintain the electrical equipment for radio and television broadcasts, concerts, sound recordings, and movies and in office and school buildings.

See How to Become One $39,870

Editors

Editors plan, review, and revise content for publication.

Bachelor's degree $51,470

Multimedia Artists and Animators

Multimedia artists and animators create animation and visual effects for television, movies, video games, and other media. They create two- and three-dimensional models and animation.

Bachelor's degree $58,510

Photographers

Photographers use their technical expertise, creativity, and composition skills to produce and preserve images that visually tell a story or record an event.

High school diploma or equivalent $29,130

Producers and Directors

Producers and directors are in charge of creating motion pictures, television shows, live theater, and other performing arts productions. They interpret a writer's script to entertain or inform an audience.

Bachelor's degree $68,440

Announcers

Announcers present music, news, and sports and may provide commentary or interview guests about these topics or other important events. Some act as a master of ceremonies (emcee) or disc jockey (DJ) at weddings, parties, or clubs.

See How to Become One $27,010

Reporters, Correspondents, and Broadcast News Analysts

Reporters, correspondents, and broadcast news analysts inform the public about news and events happening internationally, nationally, and locally. They report the news for newspapers, magazines, websites, television, and radio.

Bachelor's degree $36,000

Contacts for More Information

For more information about camera operators and film and video editors, visit

This chapter provides clear insight in the current state of Cinematographers jobs - the next chapter covers how to find and apply for Cinematographers jobs.

FINDING AND APPLYING FOR Cinematographers JOBS AND EVALUATING OFFERS

Finding—and getting—a job you want can be a challenging process, but knowing more about job search methods and application techniques can increase your chances of success. And knowing how to judge the job offers you receive makes it more likely that you will end up with the best possible job.

* Where to learn About Job Openings
* Job Search Methods
* Applying for a Job
* Job Interview Tips
* Evaluating a Job Offer

Where to Learn About Job Openings

* Personal contacts
* School career planning and placement offices
* Employers
* Classified ads:
    1. National and local newspapers
    2. Professional journals
    3. Trade magazines
    4. Internet resources
* Professional associations
* Labor unions
* State employment service offices
* Federal Government

- Community agencies
- Private employment agencies and career consultants
- Internships

Job Search Methods

Finding a job can take months of time and effort. But you can speed the process by using many methods to find job openings. Data from the Bureau of Labor Statistics suggest that people who use many job search methods find jobs faster than people who use only one or two.

Personal contacts.

Many jobs are never advertised. People get them by talking to friends, family, neighbors, acquaintances, teachers, former coworkers, and others who know of an opening. Be sure to tell people that you are looking for a job because the people you know may be some of the most effective resources for your search. To develop new contacts, join student, community, or professional organizations.

School career planning and placement offices.

High school and college placement offices help their students and alumni find jobs. Some invite recruiters to use their facilities for interviews or career fairs. They also may have lists of open jobs. Most also offer career counseling, career testing, and job search advice. Some have career resource libraries; host workshops on job search strategy, resume writing, letter writing, and effective interviewing; critique drafts of resumes; conduct mock interviews; and sponsor job fairs.

Employers.

Directly contacting employers is one of the most successful means of job hunting. Through library and Internet research, develop a list of potential employers in your desired career field. Then call these employers and check their Web sites for job openings. Web sites and business directories can tell you how to apply for a position or whom to contact. Even if no open positions are posted, do not hesitate to contact the employer: You never know when a job might become available.

Consider asking for an informational interview with people working in the career you want to learn more. Ask them how they got started, what they like and dislike about the work, what type of qualifications are necessary for the job, and what type of personality succeeds in that position. In addition to giving you career information, they may be able to put you in contact with other people who might hire you, and they can keep you in mind if a position opens up.

Classified ads.
The "Help Wanted" ads in newspapers and the Internet list numerous jobs, and many people find work by responding to these ads. But when using classified ads, keep the following in mind:

- Follow all leads to find a job; do not rely solely on the classifieds.
- Answer ads promptly, because openings may be filled quickly, even before the ad stops appearing in the paper.
- Read the ads every day, particularly the Sunday edition, which usually includes the most listings.
- Keep a record of all ads to which you have responded, including the specific skills, educational background, and personal qualifications required for the position.

Internet resources.
The Internet includes many job hunting Web sites with job listings. Some job boards provide National listings of all kinds; others are local. Some relate to a specific type of work; others are general. To find good prospects, begin with an Internet search using keywords related to the job you want. Also look for the sites of related professional associations.

Also consider checking Internet forums, also called message boards. These are online discussion groups where anyone may post and read messages. Use forums specific to your profession or to career-related topics to post questions or messages and to read about the job searches or career experiences of other people.

In online job databases, remember that job listings may be posted by field or discipline, so begin your search using keywords. Many Web sites allow job seekers to post their resumes online for free.

Professional associations. Many professions have associations that offer employment information, including career planning, educational programs, job listings, and job placement. To use these services, associations usually require that you be a member; information can be obtained directly from an association through the Internet, by telephone, or by mail.

Labor unions.

Labor unions provide various employment services to members and potential members, including apprenticeship programs that teach a specific trade or skill. Contact the appropriate labor union or State apprenticeship council for more information.

State employment service offices.

The State employment service, sometimes called the Job Service, operates in coordination with the U.S. Department of Labor's Employment and Training Administration. Local offices, found nationwide, help job seekers to find jobs and help employers to find qualified workers at no cost to either. To find the office nearest you, look in the State government telephone listings under "Job Service" or "Employment."

Job matching and referral.

At the State employment service office, an interviewer will determine if you are "job ready" or if you need help from counseling and testing services to assess your occupational aptitudes and interests and to help you choose and prepare for a career. After you are job ready, you may examine available job listings and select openings that interest you. A staff member can then describe the job openings in detail and arrange for interviews with prospective employers.

Services for special groups.

By law, veterans are entitled to priority job placement at State employment service centers. If you are a veteran, a veterans' employment representative can inform you of available assistance and help you to deal with problems.

State employment service offices also refer people to opportunities available under the Workforce Investment Act (WIA) of 1998. Educational and career services and referrals are provided to employers and job seekers, including adults, dislocated workers, and youth. These programs help to prepare people to participate in the State's workforce, increase their employment and earnings potential, improve their educational and occupational skills, and reduce their dependency on welfare.

Federal Government.

Information on obtaining a position with the Federal Government is available from the U.S. Office of Personnel Management (OPM) through USAJOBS, the Federal Government's official employment information system. This resource for locating and applying for job opportunities can be accessed through the Internet at http://www.usajobs.opm.gov or through an interactive voice response telephone system at (703) 724-1850 or TDD (978) 461-8404. These numbers are not toll free, and charges may result.

Community agencies.

Many nonprofit organizations, including religious institutions and vocational rehabilitation agencies, offer counseling, career development, and job placement services, generally targeted to a particular group, such as women, youths, minorities, ex-offenders, or older workers.

Private employment agencies and career consultants.

Private agencies can save you time and they will contact employers who otherwise might be difficult to locate. But these agencies may charge for their services. Most operate on a commission basis, charging a percentage of the first-year salary paid to a successful applicant. You or the hiring company will pay the fee. Find out the exact cost and who is responsible for paying associated fees before using the service. When determining if the service is worth the cost, consider any guarantees that the agency offers.

Internships.

Many people find jobs with business and organizations with whom they have interned or volunteered. Look for internships and volunteer opportunities on job boards, career centers, and company and association Web sites, but also check community service organizations and volunteer opportunity databases. Some internships and long-term volunteer positions come with stipends and all provide experience and the chance to meet employers and other good networking contacts.

APPLYING FOR A CINEMATOGRAPHERS JOB

After you have found some jobs that interest you, the next step is to apply for them. You will almost always need to complete resumes or application forms and cover letters. Later, you will probably need to go on interviews to meet with employers face to face.

Resumes and application forms.

Resumes and application forms give employers written evidence of your qualifications and skills. The goal of these documents is to prove—as clearly and directly as possible—how your qualifications match the job's requirements. Do this by highlighting the experience, accomplishments, education, and skills that most closely fit the job you want.

Gathering information.

Resumes and application forms both include the same information. As a first step, gather the following facts:

- Contact information, including your name, mailing address, e-mail address (if you have one you check often), and telephone number.
- Type of work or specific job you are seeking or a qualifications summary, which describes your best skills and experience in just a few lines.
- Education, including school name and its city and State, months and years of attendance, highest grade completed or diploma or degree awarded, and major subject or subjects studied. Also consider listing courses and awards that might be relevant to the position. Include a grade point average if you think it would help in getting the job.
- Experience, paid and volunteer. For each job, include the job title, name and location of employer, and dates of employment. Briefly describe your job duties and major accomplishments. In a resume, use phrases instead of sentences to describe your work; write, for example, "Supervised 10 children" instead of writing "I supervised 10 children."
- Special skills. You might list computer skills, proficiency in foreign languages, achievements, or and membership in organizations in a separate section.
- References. Be ready to provide references if requested. Good references could be former employers, coworkers, or teachers or anyone else who can describe your abilities and job-related traits. You will be asked to provide contact information for the people you

choose.

Throughout the application or resume, focus on accomplishments that relate most closely to the job you want. You can even use the job announcement as a guide, using some of the same words and phrases to describe your work and education.

Look for concrete examples that show your skills. When describing your work experience, for instance, you might say that you increased sales by 10 percent, finished a task in half the usual time, or received three letters of appreciation from customers.

Choosing a format.

After gathering the information you want to present, the next step is to put it in the proper format. In an application form, the format is set. Just fill in the blanks. But make sure you fill it out completely and follow all instructions. Do not omit any requested information. Consider making a copy of the form before filling it out, in case you make a mistake and have to start over. If possible, have someone else look over the form before submitting it.

In a resume, there are many ways of organizing the information you want to include, but the most important information should usually come first. Most applicants list their past jobs in reverse chronological order, describing their most recent employment first and working backward. But some applicants use a functional format, organizing their work experience under headings that describe their major skills. They then include a brief work history section that lists only job titles, employers, and dates of employment. Still other applicants choose a format that combines these two approaches in some way. Choose the style that best showcases your skills and experience.

Whatever format you choose, keep your resume short. Many experts recommend that new workers use a one-page resume. Avoid long blocks of text and italicized material. Consider using bullets to highlight duties or key accomplishments.

Before submitting your resume, make sure that it is easy to read. Are the headings clear and consistently formatted with bold or some other style of type? Is the type face large enough? Then, ask at least two people to proofread the resume for spelling and other errors and make sure you use your computer's spell checker.

Keep in mind that many employers scan resumes into databases, which they then search for specific keywords or phrases. The keywords are usually nouns referring to experience, education, personal characteristics, or industry buzz words. Identify keywords by reading tasks and qualifications in the job ad; use these same words in your resume. For example, if the role includes customer service tasks, use the words "customer service" on your resume. Scanners sometimes misread paper resumes, which could mean some of your keywords don't get into the database. So, if you know that your resume will be scanned, and you have the option, e-mail an electronic version. If you must submit a paper resume, make it scannable by using a simple font and avoiding underlines, italics, and graphics. It is also a good idea to send a traditionally formatted resume along with your scannable resume, with a note on each marking its purpose.

Resume and KSA (knowledge, skills & abilities) tips:

Pay Attention to Keywords

Whether you're writing your first resume, updating an existing one, or answering a position's Knowledges, Skills, and Abilities (KSA's), stop and think about which keywords you need to add. You could be the most qualified person for the position, but you could be lost in a sea of applicants without the right keywords.

A Single Keyword Communicates Multiple Skills and Qualifications

When a recruiter reads the keyword "analyst," he or she might assume you have experience in collecting data, evaluating effectiveness, and researching and developing new processes. Just one keyword can have tremendous power and deliver a huge message.

Study Job Announcements

This is the best way to determine important keywords. Review several job announcements and their questions for your ideal position. The jobs don't have to be in your geographic target area. The idea is to find skills, experience, education and other credentials important in your field. You will probably find keywords frequently mentioned by different agencies. Focus on the "requirements," "skills" or "qualifications" sections of job ads, and look for "buzzwords" and desirable credentials for your ideal job.

Be Concise

Don't confuse telling your story with creating your autobiography. Recruiters are inundated with applications and are faced with weeding out the good from the bad. The first step involves quickly skimming through submissions and eliminating candidates who clearly are not qualified. Therefore, your application needs to pass the skim test. Look at your resume and/or KSA's and ask yourself:

- Can a hiring manager see my main credentials within 10 to 15 seconds?
- Does critical information jump off the page?
- Do I effectively sell myself on the top quarter of the first page?

The Sales Pitch

Because applications are quickly skimmed during the first pass, it is crucial your resume and KSA's get right to work selling your credentials. Your key selling points need to be prominently displayed at the top of the first page of the resume and directly address each question asked in the KSA section. For example, if an advanced degree is an important qualification, it shouldn't be buried at the end of a four-page resume. If a KSA question asks about your writing ability, immediately detail your experience instead of enjoyment of it.

Use an Editor's Eye

Many workers are proud of their careers and feel the information on a resume should reflect everything they've accomplished. However, a resume shouldn't contain every detail and KSA's should only address the question at hand. So be judicious. If your college days are far behind you, does it really matter that you pledged a fraternity or delivered pizza? The editing step will be difficult if you are holding on to your past for emotional reasons.

Use Numbers to Highlight Your Accomplishments

If you were a recruiter looking at a resume or an answer to a KSA, which of the following entries would impress you more:

- Wrote news releases.
- Wrote 25 news releases in a three-week period under daily deadlines.

Clearly the second statement carries more weight. Why? Because it uses numbers to quantify the writer's accomplishment, giving it a context that helps the interviewer understand the degree of difficulty involved in the task. Numbers are powerful resume tools that will help your accomplishments draw the attention they deserve from prospective employers. With just a little thought, you can find effective ways to quantify your successes on your resume.

Think Money

For-profit, nonprofit, and government organizations alike are and always will be concerned about money. So as you contemplate your accomplishments and prepare to present them on your resume or in your KSA's, think about ways you've saved money, earned money, or managed money in your internships, part-time jobs and extracurricular activities so far. A few possibilities that might appear on a typical college student's resume:

- Identified, researched and recommended a new Internet Service Provider, cutting the company's online costs by 15 percent.
- Wrote prospect letter that has brought in more than $25,000 in donations to date.
- Managed a student organization budget of more than $7,000.

Think Time

You've heard the old saying, "Time is money," and it's true. Companies and organizations are constantly looking for ways to save time and do things more efficiently. They're also necessarily concerned about meeting deadlines, both internal and external. So whatever you can do on your resume or in your KSA's to show that you can save time, make time or manage time will grab your reader's immediate attention. Here are some time-oriented entries that might appear on a typical college student's resume:

- Assisted with twice-monthly payroll activities, ensuring employees were paid as expected and on time.
- Attended high school basketball games, interviewed players and coaches afterward, and composed 750-word articles by an 11 p.m. deadline.
- Suggested procedures that decreased average order-processing time from 10 minutes to five minutes.

Cover letters.
When sending a resume, most people include a cover letter to introduce

themselves to the prospective employer. Most cover letters are no more than three short paragraphs. Your cover letter should capture the employer's attention, follow a business letter format, and usually should include the following information:

- Name and address of the specific person to whom the letter is addressed.
- Reason for your interest in the company or position.
- Your main qualifications for the position.
- Request for an interview.
- Your home and work telephone numbers.

If you send a scannable resume, you should also include a scannable cover letter, which avoids graphics, fancy fonts, italics, and underlines.

As with your resume, it may be helpful to look for examples on the Internet or in books at your local library or bookstore, but be sure not to copy letters directly from other sources.

CINEMATOGRAPHERS JOB INTERVIEW TIPS

An interview gives you the opportunity to showcase your qualifications to an employer, so it pays to be well prepared. The following information provides some helpful hints.

Preparation:

- Learn about the organization.
- Have a specific job or jobs in mind.
- Review your qualifications for the job.
- Be ready to briefly describe your experience, showing how it relates it the job.
- Be ready to answer broad questions, such as "Why should I hire you?" "Why do you want this job?" "What are your strengths and weaknesses?"
- Practice an interview with a friend or relative.

Personal appearance:

- Be well groomed.
- Dress appropriately.
- Do not chew gum or smoke.

The interview:

- Be early.
- Learn the name of your interviewer and greet him or her with a firm handshake.
- Use good manners with everyone you meet.
- Relax and answer each question concisely.
- Use proper English—avoid slang.
- Be cooperative and enthusiastic.
- Use body language to show interest—use eye contact and don't slouch.
- Ask questions about the position and the organization, but avoid questions whose answers can easily be found on the company Web site.
- Also avoid asking questions about salary and benefits unless a job offer is made.
- Thank the interviewer when you leave and shake hands.

*   Send a short thank you note.

Information to bring to an interview:

*   Social Security card.
*   Government-issued identification (driver's license).
*   Resume or application. Although not all employers require a resume, you should be able to furnish the interviewer information about your education, training, and previous employment.
*   References. Employers typically require three references. Get permission before using anyone as a reference. Make sure that they will give you a good reference. Try to avoid using relatives as references.
*   Transcripts. Employers may require an official copy of transcripts to verify grades, coursework, dates of attendance, and highest grade completed or degree awarded.

EVALUATING A CINEMATOGRAPHERS JOB OFFER

Once you receive a job offer, you must decide if you want the job. Fortunately, most organizations will give you a few days to accept or reject an offer.

There are many issues to consider when assessing a job offer.
- Will the organization be a good place to work?
- Will the job be interesting?
- Are there opportunities for advancement?
- Is the salary fair?
- Does the employer offer good benefits?

Now is the time to ask the potential employer about these issues—and to do some checking on your own?

The organization.

Background information on an organization can help you to decide whether it is a good place for you to work. Factors to consider include the organization's business or activity, financial condition, age, size, and location.

You generally can get background information on an organization, particularly a large organization, on its Internet site or by telephoning its public relations office. A public company's annual report to the stockholders tells about its corporate philosophy, history, products or services, goals, and financial status. Most government agencies can furnish reports that describe their programs and missions. Press releases, company newsletters or magazines, and recruitment brochures also can be useful. Ask the organization for any other items that might interest a prospective employee. If possible, speak to current or former employees of the organization.

Background information on the organization may be available at your public or school library. If you cannot get an annual report, check the library for reference directories that may provide basic facts about the company, such as earnings, products and services, and number of employees. Some directories widely available in libraries either in print or as online databases include:

- Dun & Bradstreet's Million Dollar Directory
- Standard and Poor's Register of Corporations

- Mergent's Industrial Review (formerly Moody's Industrial Manual)
- Thomas Register of American Manufacturers
- Ward's Business Directory

Stories about an organization in magazines and newspapers can tell a great deal about its successes, failures, and plans for the future. You can identify articles on a company by looking under its name in periodical or computerized indexes in libraries, or by using one of the Internet's search engines. However, it probably will not be useful to look back more than 2 or 3 years.

The library also may have government publications that present projections of growth for the industry in which the organization is classified. Long-term projections of employment and output for detailed industries, covering the entire U.S. economy, are developed by the Bureau of Labor Statistics and revised every 2 years. (See the Career Guide to Industries, online at www.bls.gov/oco/cg.) Trade magazines also may include articles on the trends for specific industries.

Career centers at colleges and universities often have information on employers that is not available in libraries. Ask a career center representative how to find out about a particular organization.

During your research consider the following questions:

- Does the organization's business or activity match your own interests and beliefs?
-
- It is easier to apply yourself to the work if you are enthusiastic about what the organization does.
-
- How will the size of the organization affect you?

Large firms generally offer a greater variety of training programs and career paths, more managerial levels for advancement, and better employee benefits than do small firms. Large employers also may have more advanced technologies. However, many jobs in large firms tend to be highly specialized.

Jobs in small firms may offer broader authority and responsibility, a closer working relationship with top management, and a chance to clearly see your contribution to the success of the organization.

Should you work for a relatively new organization or one that is well established?

New businesses have a high failure rate, but for many people, the excitement of helping to create a company and the potential for sharing in its success more than offset the risk of job loss. However, it may be just as exciting and rewarding to work for a young firm that already has a foothold on success.

The job

Even if everything else about the job is attractive, you will be unhappy if you dislike the day-to-day work. Determining in advance whether you will like the work may be difficult. However, the more you find out about the job before accepting or rejecting the offer, the more likely you are to make the right choice. Consider the following questions:

Where is the job located?

If the job is in another section of the country, you need to consider the cost of living, the availability of housing and transportation, and the quality of educational and recreational facilities in that section of the country. Even if the job location is in your area, you should consider the time and expense of commuting.

Does the work match your interests and make good use of your skills?

The duties and responsibilities of the job should be explained in enough detail to answer this question.

How important is the job to the company or organization?

An explanation of where you fit in the organization and how you are supposed to contribute to its overall goals should give you an idea of the job's importance.

What will the hours be?

Most jobs involve regular hours—for example, 40 hours a week, during the day, Monday through Friday. Other jobs require night, weekend, or holiday work. In addition, some jobs routinely require overtime to meet deadlines or sales or production goals, or to better serve customers. Consider the effect that the work hours will have on your personal life.

How long do most people who enter this job stay with the company?

High turnover can mean dissatisfaction with the nature of the work or something else about the job.

Opportunities offered by employers. A good job offers you opportunities to learn new skills, increase your earnings, and rise to positions of greater authority, responsibility, and prestige. A lack of opportunities can dampen interest in the work and result in frustration and boredom.

The company should have a training plan for you.

What valuable new skills does the company plan to teach you?

The employer should give you some idea of promotion possibilities within the organization. What is the next step on the career ladder? If you have to wait for a job to become vacant before you can be promoted, how long does this usually take? When opportunities for advancement do arise, will you compete with applicants from outside the company? Can you apply for jobs for which you qualify elsewhere within the organization, or are mobility within the firm limited?

Salaries and benefits.

When an employer makes a job offer, information about earnings and benefits are usually included. You will want to research to determine if the offer is fair. If you choose to negotiate for higher pay and better benefits, objective research will help you strengthen your case.

You should also look for additional information, specifically tailored to your job offer and circumstances. Try to find family, friends, or acquaintances that recently were hired in similar jobs. Ask your teachers and the staff in placement offices about starting pay for graduates with your qualifications. Help-wanted ads in newspapers sometimes give salary ranges for similar positions. Check the library or your school's career center for salary surveys such as those conducted by the National Association of Colleges and Employers or various professional associations.

If you are considering the salary and benefits for a job in another geographic area, make allowances for differences in the cost of living, which may be significantly higher in a large metropolitan area than in a smaller city, town, or rural area.

You also should learn the organization's policy regarding overtime. Depending on the job, you may or may not be exempt from laws requiring the employer to compensate you for overtime. Find out how many hours you will be expected to work each week and whether you receive overtime pay or compensatory time off for working more than the specified number of hours in a week.

Also take into account that the starting salary is just that—the start. Your salary should be reviewed on a regular basis; many organizations do it every year. How much can you expect to earn after 1, 2, or 3 or more years? An employer cannot be specific about the amount of pay if it includes commissions and bonuses.

Benefits also can add a lot to your base pay, but they vary widely. Find out exactly what the benefit package includes and how much of the cost you must bear.

WHAT TO EXPECT FROM THE OTHER SIDE OF THE TABLE...

HIRING THE BEST Cinematographers

This chapter is all about clarity of the total hiring process – for you, your manager and your candidates.

You will need or encounter a Great Process to Hire the Best. Computers and equipment are wonderful tools, but people make the difference. Hiring the Best makes it clear just how valuable it is to hire and work with the best. The mistakes you will avoid make the investment very valuable. Hiring the Best provides you with a process that reduces trial and error in recruiting a lot, but still ensures that you will be able to hire the best.

This chapter guides you to how to perform a truly in-depth hiring process and interview for candidates. The process will allow you and your company to select the best candidates for key positions.

You will be able to use the materials shown here as an outstanding tool, giving you insight into the candidates experience, performance history, and growth allowing you to determine what they are capable of today and in the future.

This will, in short, let you go from hoping your next hire works out to being confident your next hire will be a star.

Before you make your next hire, use this Guide.

THE INTERVIEW AND SELECTION PROCESS

A position description, observing the job being performed, and interviewing the previous and current holders of the job and the immediate supervisor will be helpful in determining the competencies required and the performance standard.

Asking a series of questions will help you in establishing the technical competencies. Ask questions such as:

- What would the "perfect" candidate's competencies and skills look like;
- What will a person in this job have to do on a regular basis to

succeed;
- What are the necessary competencies and skills the person will need in order to achieve the desired results of the position;
- How will a person hired for this job know he or she is succeeding, and
- Why have people left this job in the past?

After you have analyzed the job and developed several technical competencies, list the top five most important technical competencies the candidate MUST have to succeed in the job.

Remember when developing your interview questions to keep the questions open-ended, simple, direct and specific. Base all the questions on the role its top five technical competencies.

Avoid questions that require overly specific knowledge.

Below is a sample Technical Competency Assessment Guide for use in determining the technical competencies and developing relevant interview questions.

Step 1

Technical Competencies Assessment Guide

Job Title: _____

1. Analyze Technical Aspects of Job. (Answer questions and list competencies in the space.)

*   What would the "perfect" candidate's competencies and skills look like?
*
*   What will a person in this job have to do on a regular basis to succeed?
*
*   What are the necessary competencies and skills the person will need in order to achieve the desired results of the position?
*
*   How will a person hired for this job know he or she is succeeding?
*
*   Why have people left this job in the past?

2. List the top five most important technical competencies the candidate MUST have to succeed in the job.

    1.

    2.

    3.

    4.

    5.

3. Develop a Technical Question for Each of the Five Required Technical Competencies.

*   Base all your questions on the technical competencies you listed above.
*   Keep the questions open-ended, simple, direct and specific.
*   Avoid questions that require a specific knowledge of your division.
*   Ask for assistance developing technical questions if you are not the

technical expert.

Step 2

Determine the Customer Service Focused Competencies of the Job

A large percentage of employees who did not succeed in a position had the technical skills but did not have the customer service focused skills required for the job. Identifying the customer service focused competencies needed to successfully perform the job and determining if the candidate possesses those competencies is critical. For example, an individual working in a receptionist position will need to be flexible and unflappable in order to handle the pressure of multiple phone calls and simultaneous visitors. They also need some degree of friendliness for welcoming the public and some degree of extroversion, since most people calling an organization would like to be met by someone with enthusiasm.

Assessing customer service focused competencies during the interview process is something we may not be typically used to doing as managers. We are experienced in determining if the candidate has the technical skills and abilities to perform the job. But in order to get the BEST candidate for the position, customer service focused competencies need to be determined and assessed also.

To determine what customer service focused competencies are needed for the position, questions similar to those asked to determine the technical competencies should be answered:
- What would the "perfect" candidate's customer service focused competencies look like;
- What will a person in this job have to do on a regular basis to succeed;
- What are the necessary customer service focused competencies the person will need in order to achieve the desired results of the position;
- How will a person hired for this job know he or she is meeting the customer service focused expectations; and
- Related to customer service reasons, why have people left this job in the past?

As you think about the job vacancy you need to fill, focus on the customer service focused competencies or behaviors that an individual needs to exhibit in order to succeed in this job.

Depending on the specific job under consideration, customer service focused characteristics, such as paying attention to detail, being self-motivated, getting along with others, having leadership qualities, and being tolerant of stressful events, are examples of the skills critical to success on the job.

Below you will find five descriptive elements of personality to assist you in determining customer service focused competencies. Descriptive words have been added to give you ideas and help you determine what behaviors are required for the position.

Towards the end of this document, you will find a list of questions to correspond to each personality factor. These questions can be used to develop the examination portion of the recruiting announcement or they can be used in the interview process.

The five descriptive elements of personality are Responsible, Likeable, Believable, Outgoing and Unflappable.

Definitions:

Responsible.

The ability to organize or schedule people, tasks, and self; to develop realistic action plans while remaining sensitive to time constraints and resource availability; and having a well developed sense of ethics and integrity. Characterized by high levels of responsibility and behaviors these employees are controlled, disciplined, precise, persistent, and businesslike. Their behavior is consistent, scrupulous, and reliable, and their work is purposeful, highly systematic, and well organized. They approach life as a series of tasks to be accomplished and goals to be reached.

Descriptors: detail-oriented; quality-focused; high-integrity; responsible; trustworthy; dependable; cost-conscious; exact; disciplined; committed; cautious; casual; easygoing.

Likeable.

Describes a person's ability to modify their behavioral style to respond to the needs of others while maintaining one's own objectives and sense of dignity. In the moderate to high range of likeability, we find sympathetic, helpful, and understanding individuals. They are agreeable, compassionate, thoughtful, and kind. They appear to accept things as they are, nurture others, and are obviously friendly and caring people.

Descriptors: amicable; accommodating; supportive; helpful; compromising; collaborative; friendly; empathetic; empowering; congenial; easygoing.

Believable.

Capable of eliciting belief or trust. In the middle to low range of believable thinking, we find people who are open, willing to reexamine tenets and consider new ideas. They are capable of reasonable levels of professional and personal risk taking and are willing to work outside their "comfort zone." Highly believable people can be described as practical, predictable and conventional, willing to follow procedures without question. They often form the emotional "back bone" of an organization.

Descriptors: creative; original; flexible; spontaneous; open-to-new-ideas; independent; curious; untraditional; venturesome; uninhibited; conventional; down-to-earth; concrete; traditional; practical; methodical; systematic.

Outgoing.

Describes the ability to work with people in such a manner as to build high morale and group commitments to goals and objectives. Individuals in the moderately high range of extroversion are upbeat, positive, and energetic. They tend to be enterprising, cheerful, and appropriately assertive. They demonstrate leadership, team-building capability, and are able to coach or facilitate a work team's progress. Individuals who are moderately introverted are often viewed as self-contained, generally well balanced, and able to work well either alone or in small groups.

Descriptors: active; outgoing; dominant; forceful; enthusiastic; assertive; persuasive; energizing; entrepreneurial; ambitious; risk-taking; self-contained; task-oriented; quiet; restrained; formal; unassuming; reserved; thoughtful.

Unflappable.

The ability to maintain a mature, problem-solving attitude while dealing with a range of stressful conditions, such as interpersonal conflict, hazardous conditions, personal rejection, hostility, or time demands. At moderately high levels of stress tolerance we find relaxed, secure, and hardy individuals who are poised and adaptive in a wide range of situations. They are steady, realistic, self-reliant, and able to cope effectively across a wide range of situations and circumstances. They demonstrate maturity that is not necessarily related to age, but to the ability to maintain a clear perspective under stressful conditions as well as those that elicit little or no stress.

Descriptors: calm; well adjusted; secure; even-tempered; self-assured; unflappable; resilient; poised; composed; self-confident; optimistic.

CUSTOMER SERVICE FOCUSED BEHAVIORS ASSESSMENT GUIDE

Job Title: _____

A.   List the most typical Customer Service Focused behaviors required on this job on a daily basis. Use the previously identified personality factors to help you.

- Responsible – detail-oriented; quality-focused; high-integrity; responsible; trustworthy; dependable; cost conscious; exact; disciplined; committed; cautious; casual; easygoing.

- Likeable – amicable; accommodating; supportive; helpful; compromising; collaborative; friendly; empathetic; empowering; congenial; easygoing.

- Believable – creative; original; flexible; spontaneous; open-to-new-ideas; independent; curious; untraditional; venturesome; uninhibited; conventional; down-to-earth; concrete; traditional; practical; methodical; systematic.

- Outgoing – active; outgoing; dominant; forceful; enthusiastic; assertive; persuasive; energizing; entrepreneurial; ambitious; risk-taking; self-contained; task-oriented; quiet; restrained; formal; unassuming; reserved; thoughtful.

- Unflappable – calm; well-adjusted; secure; even-tempered; self-assured; unflappable; resilient; poised; composed; self-confident; optimistic.

B.   List of Customer Service Focused Behaviors

1.

2.

3.

4.

5.

C.   Develop a Question for Each of the Customer Service Focused Behaviors

1.

2.

3.

4.

5.

Step 3

Develop Interview Questions to Assess Both Technical and Customer Service Focused Competencies

Decide how long the interviews will be and select a reasonable number of questions to ask. In a half-hour interview, only about 5 behavioral-based questions can comfortably be asked. If five questions are asked, at least two of them should be customer service-type questions, depending upon the type of job.

Always ask open-ended questions. Ask, "This job involves dealing with difficult customers. Think of a time when you had to deal with a difficult customer and tell us what you did." Don't ask, "Have you ever dealt with difficult customers?" You probably will get an answer like, "Yes, I work with difficult customers all the time." But it won't tell you HOW the individual works with difficult customers. If you feel the candidate is making up an answer, or is giving you a "canned" answer, ask a probing question or two to get more detail. "What exactly did you say to the customer to get them to stop yelling?" Generally, if they have read a book on "most commonly asked interview questions" and memorized an answer, or are making up the situation, a probing question will generally fluster them and they will not be as confident in giving an answer. You can ask for the candidate to think of another example to use in answering the question.

Using the list of most important tasks you developed during the review of the Position Description, develop open-ended questions to determine if the candidate has the technical skills necessary for the job. Only ask technical questions that relate to that particular job. Don't ask a question about using equipment if they don't use that equipment to do their job.

Using the list of customer service focused skills you identified from the position description are needed to do the job, develop open-ended questions to determine the candidate's customer service focused competencies.

There is a list of sample interview questions at the end of this document to help you.

They are arranged by the five personality factors identified above.

Step 4

Conducting the Interview

Have an interview panel of at least two managers/supervisors; some managers may also wish to include a non-management employee with special knowledge of the position duties as part of a panel.

If you choose to include a non-management employee on your interview panel, be sure to discuss interviewing procedures and confidentiality of candidate information with the employee prior to the interviews. It is encouraged that all interview panels be as diverse as possible.

Before the interview starts, establish the criteria used for scoring and then meet with the interview panel to discuss the process and review the questions and criteria used for scoring.

Welcome the candidate and establish rapport by introducing them to the members of the interview panel. Ask easy questions such as "Did you have any difficulty finding the office?" or "Would you like a glass of water before we begin?" Give a brief explanation of the organization or section and show the organization chart so they understand how this position fits within the organization. If you have handed the position description and organization chart out while they waited for the interview to start, ask if they have any questions about the position or organization. Explaining the interview process can also help ease a candidate's nervousness and also gives them information about the process, including, approximate length of the interview, the interview will be a series of prepared questions asked by the interview panel designed to get to know the candidate, and the panel will be taking notes during the interview.

Transition into the main purpose of the interview by saying, "Let's get a bit more focused and start asking the interview questions." Even though the interview process is accomplished through a panel, one person should act as "facilitator" and make sure the interview stays focused. Some candidates tend to wander, give "canned" speeches, or simply try to deliver a monologue. In such cases, you need to diplomatically interrupt and redirect the candidate to the question at hand. You might simply say, "I think we've gotten a little off target here. Let me restate my question."

To clarify a response or to get a candidate to give specific examples you can ask, "Please give me a specific example about when you..." Because behavior-based questions require specific examples to answer them successfully, sometimes a candidate will need to think for a few seconds to come up with an appropriate example. You may have to wait 30, 60, or even 90 seconds for the candidate to start answering the question. Resist the temptation to talk during this silence! It takes time to recall specific behavioral examples that clearly answer your questions and you want the candidate to do their best during the interview. An option available to the hiring manager is to hand out the list of questions to the candidates a few minutes before the interview starts, so the candidate can start thinking of specific examples ahead of time and organizing their thoughts.

If an answer does not give you the information you need to rate the candidate's answer, use open-ended probes such as:

"Could you review your role in...?"
"Please describe how you..."
"What happened after...?"

If after the first or second try to get an answer more relevant to the question move on to the next question.
After each interview take a few minutes for the panel members to summarize their thoughts and score the questions, or complete the rating process.

Affirmative Action

Organizations value diversity in the workplace. Every effort will be made to reach out to the broadest possible labor market. All employment decisions will be based on the most suitable candidate relative to a position, while taking into consideration Affirmative Action goals.

Step 5

Background and Reference Checks

The final stage of the hiring process is the background and reference checks. The Human Resources Background Investigator will verify information provided by the applicant by contacting former and current supervisors, persons listed by the candidate as references, and others who are thought to be able to provide information about the competencies of a candidate.

The Background Investigator listens for subtle innuendoes and long pauses after posing questions, and will evaluate whether the individual giving the reference sounds like he/she is struggling to carefully select each word. In these instances, more specific probing questions will be asked.

Occasionally, a finalist will indicate they do not wish you to contact their current employer. In these cases, you need to explain that the organization needs to contact this employer to assist with the hiring decision and that we don't hire anyone without completing a background and reference check with the current employer.

Making a Job Offer

When you have identified the candidate to whom you would like to make a job offer based on the information gathered through the application, examination, interview, evaluation of background and references, and you have the approval of your supervisor, and the Director or Deputy Director, you may contact that candidate and offer him/her the position.

Before you contact the candidate, please work closely with Human Resources staff to verify certain information. For example,
- Classification
- Salary Range
- Rate of pay and timing of first pay increase
- Vacation accrual rate and ability to transfer vacation accruals from

another State organization
- Trial Service period
- Eligibility for Personal benefits

Confirming Job Offer Letter

Human Resources staff will send a confirming job offer letter. The letter will outline the terms of the job offer and will provide a space for the candidate to sign his or her name confirming that he/she accepts the terms of employment. This signed copy must be returned to Human Resources to document the understanding and the acceptance of the terms.

It is important that all information in this letter of confirming letter of hire be correctly stated because it is an implied employment contract.

Informing Unsuccessful Candidates

After the selected candidate formally accepts your job offer, each of the remaining candidates should be contacted to notify them that the hiring decision has been made. Human Resources can help you with this step.

If a candidate contacts you directly to ask why he or she was not hired, the best thing to do is to simply tell them that we hired the most suitable candidate for the position. If they continue to ask for information, contact your Human Resources staff for guidance in how to answer the candidate's questions.

Retention of Interview Materials

Please collect all interview and selection materials and notes and return them promptly to Human Resources.

SAMPLE CUSTOMER SERVICE FOCUSED INTERVIEW QUESTIONS

(Grouped by customer service based behaviors)

Responsible

1. Tell us about a time when the details of something you were doing were especially important. How did you attend to them?
2. Describe a time when you had to make a difficult decision on the job. What facts did you consider? How long did it take you to make a decision?
3. Jobs differ in the extent to which people work independently or as part of a team. Tell us about a time when you worked independently.
4. It is often easy to blur the distinction between confidential information and public knowledge. Have you ever been faced with this dilemma? What did you do?
5. Tell us about a time when you put in some extra effort to help move a particular project forward. How did you do it and what happened?
6. Tell us about a demanding situation in which you managed to remain calm and composed. What did you do and what was the outcome?
7. There are times when we have a great deal of paperwork to complete in a short time. How do you do to ensure your accuracy?
8. Give an example of a time you noticed a process or task that was not being done correctly. How did you discover or come to notice it, and what did you do?
9. We often have to push ourselves harder to reach a target. Give us a specific example of when you had to give yourself that extra push.
10. Tell us about a time when you achieved success through your willingness to react quickly.
11. Tell us about a time when you disagreed with a procedure or policy instituted by management. What was your reaction and how did you implement the procedure or policy?
12. What kinds of measures have you taken to make sure all of the small details of a project or assignment were done? Please give a specific example.
13. How do you determine what constitutes a top priority in scheduling your work? Give a specific example.
14. If I call your references, what will they say about you?
15. What are two or three examples of tasks that you do not particularly enjoy doing? Tell us how you remain motivated to complete those tasks.
16. What has been your greatest success, personally or professionally?

17. What can you tell us about yourself that you feel is unique and makes you the best candidate for this position?
18. What strengths do you have that we haven't talked about?
19. Tell us about a time when you had to review detailed reports or documents to identify a problem. How did you go about it? What did you do when you discovered a problem?
20. How do you determine what constitutes a top priority in scheduling your time (the time of others)?
21. Do you have a system for organizing your own work area? Tell us how that system helped you on the job.
22. Have you planned any conferences, workshops or retreats? What steps did you take to plan the event?

Likeable

1. Tell us about a time when you were able to build a successful relationship with a difficult person.
2. Give us an example of how you have been able to develop a close, positive relationship with one of your customers.
3. Give us an example of how you establish an atmosphere at work where others feel comfortable in communicating their ideas, feelings and concerns.
4. Describe a particularly trying customer complaint or resistance you had to handle. How did you react and what was the outcome?
5. How would you describe your management style? How do you think your subordinates perceive you?
6. Some people are difficult to work with. Tell us about a time when you encountered such a person. How did you handle it?
7. In working with people, we find that what works with one person does not work with another. Therefore, we have to be flexible in our style of relating to others. Give us a specific example of when you had to vary your work style with a particular individual. How did it work out?
8. It is important to remain composed at work and to maintain a positive outlook. Give us a specific example of when you were able to do this.
9. Having an understanding of the other person's perspective is crucial in dealing with customers. Give us an example of a time when you achieved success through attaining insight into the other person's perspective.
10. Have you ever had difficulty getting along with a co-worker? How did you handle the situation and what was the outcome?
11. Tell us about a time when you needed someone's cooperation to complete a task and the person was uncooperative. What did you do?

What was the outcome?

12. There are times when people need extra assistance with difficult projects. Give us an example of when you offered assistance to someone with whom you worked.

13. Tell us about a situation in which you became frustrated or impatient when dealing with a coworker. What did you do? What was the outcome?

14. Many jobs are team-oriented where a work group is the key to success. Give us an example of a time when you worked on a team to complete a project. How did it work? What was the outcome?

15. Tell us about a job where the atmosphere was the easiest for you to get along and function well. Describe the qualities of that work environment.

16. On occasion we may be faced with a situation that has escalated to become a confrontation. If you have had such an experience, tell me how you handled it. What was the outcome? Would you do anything differently today?

17. Describe a time when you weren't sure what a customer wanted. How did you handle the situation?

18. We don't always make decisions that everyone agrees with. Give us an example of an unpopular decision you have made. How did you communicate the decision and what was the outcome?

Believable

1. Describe your ideal supervisor.
2. What were some of the most important things you accomplished on your last job?
3. What is your management style? How do you think your subordinates perceive you?
4. Give us an example of when someone brought you a new idea, particularly one that was odd or unusual. What did you do?
5. It is important that performance and other personnel issues be addressed timely. Give examples of the type of personnel issues you've confronted and how you addressed them. Including examples of the process you used for any disciplinary action taken or grievance resolved.
6. Give us an example of how you establish an atmosphere at work where others feel comfortable in communicating their ideas, feelings and concerns.
7. Give a specific example of how you have involved subordinates in

identifying performance goals and expectations.

8. All jobs have their frustrations and problems. Describe some specific tasks or conditions that have been frustrating to you. Why were they frustrating and what did you do?

9. Jobs differ in the degree to which unexpected changes can disrupt daily responsibilities. Tell what you did and us about a time when this happened.

10. What are your standards of success in your job and how do you know when you are successful?

11. Sometimes supervisors' evaluations differ from our own. What did you do about it?

12. What do you do differently from other (_____)? Why? Give examples.

13. We don't always make decisions that everyone agrees with. Give us an example of an unpopular decision you made. How did you communicate the decision and what was the outcome?

14. Describe a situation in which you received a new procedure or instructions with which you disagreed. What did you do?

15. Describe a situation in which you had to translate a broad or general directive from superiors into individual performance expectations. How did you do this and what were the results?

16. Give an example of how you monitor the progress your employees are making on projects or tasks you delegated.

Outgoing

1. Describe a time when you were able to effectively communicate a difficult or unpleasant idea to a superior.

2. Tell us about a time when you had to motivate a group of people to get an important job done. What did you do, what was the outcome?

3. Tell us about a time when you delayed responding to a situation until you had time to review the facts, even though there was pressure to act quickly.

4. There are times when we need to insist on doing something a certain way. Give us the details surrounding a situation when you had to insist on doing something "your way". What was the outcome?

5. On occasion, we have to be firm and assertive in order to achieve a desired result. Tell us about a time when you had to do that.

6. Being successful is hard work. Tell us about a specific achievement when you had to work especially hard to attain the success you desired.

7. In job situations you may be pulled in many different directions at

once. Tell us about a time when you had to respond to this type of situation. How did you manage yourself?

8. Many of us have had co-workers or managers who tested our patience. Tell us about a time when you restrained yourself to avoid conflict with a co-worker or supervisor. (restrained)
9. In working with people, we find that what works with one person does not work with another. Therefore, we have to be flexible in our style of relating to others. Give us a specific example of when you had to vary your work style with a particular individual. How did it work out?
10. Describe some particularly trying customer complaints or resistance you have had to handle. How did you react? What was the outcome?
11. Have you ever had difficulty getting along with co-workers? How did you handle the situation and what was the outcome?
12. Tell us about a time when you needed someone's cooperation to complete a task and the person was uncooperative. What did you do? What was the outcome?
13. Tell us about a situation in which you became frustrated or impatient when dealing with a coworker. What did you do? What was the outcome?
14. Sooner or later we all have to deal with a customer who has unreasonable demands. Think of a time when you had to handle unreasonable requests. What did you do and what was the outcome?
15. Tell us about a time when you were effective in handling a customer complaint. Why were you effective? What was the outcome?
16. How do you know if your customers are satisfied?

Unflappable

1. There are times when we all have to deal with deadlines and it can be stressful. Tell us about a time when you felt pressured at work and how you coped with it.
2. Give us an example of a demanding situation when you were able to maintain your composure while others got upset.
3. On occasion, we experience conflict with our superiors. Describe such a situation and tell us how you handled the conflict. What was the outcome?
4. We have to find ways to tolerate and work with difficult people. Tell us about a time when you have done this.
5. Many times, a job requires you to quickly shift your attention from one task to the next. Tell us about a time at work when you had to change focus onto another task. What was the outcome?
6. Tell us about a time when you received accurate, negative feedback

by a co-worker, boss, or customer. How did you handle the evaluation? How did it affect your work?

7. Give us an example of when you felt overly sensitive to feedback or criticism. How did you handle your feelings?
8. Give us an example of when you made a presentation to an uninterested or hostile audience. How did it turn out?
9. Tell us about a time when you put in some extra effort to help move a project forward. How did you do that? What happened?
10. Describe suggestions you have made to improve work procedures. How did it turn out?

INTERVIEWING Cinematographers

A Practical Guide for Selecting

THE INTERVIEW PROCESS

Planning

Time spent planning will ensure the interview process proceeds smoothly and that you obtain the information needed to assess the candidates. You should:

*   Review the position description and qualification requirements (refer to the vacancy announcement).
*   Thoroughly review all candidate applications. Ask yourself: – What are the strengths/weaknesses of this candidate?
*   What is the candidate's relevant skills/experience? – Does the education fit the job requirements?
*   Is there evidence of the ability to communicate with individuals and groups from diverse backgrounds in a variety of situations?
*   Is there evidence of the ability to lead and accomplish work through others?
*   Decide who you will interview. Although you are not required to interview all candidates, think about the perception of other candidates if you interview only one person.
*   Formulate questions and write them down. This will help ensure you ask all candidates the same questions.
*   Allow 1-2 hours for the interview.

Confirming/Scheduling Interview

Selecting officials are encouraged to confirm scheduled interviews with applicants in writing.

Conducting the Interview

After welcoming the candidate, spend a few minutes chatting informally. It will help you both relax.

- Give a brief overview of the job and mission of the organization.
- Ask questions and listen.
- Probe for additional information. Ask the candidate to elaborate on or clarify what was just said. (Although it is important that you write down a list of questions before you begin the interviews, you are not prohibited from asking additional questions.)

Indirect probing is also an effective way to elicit more information. If you are silent for a few seconds after the candidate responds, that may allow them time to think of additional things to say; or you may use neutral phrases, such as: I see, or, oh? That may prompt the candidate to elaborate further. The point is that in this phase of the interview, it is the candidate who should be doing most of the talking.

- Take notes, but don't try to capture every word. It's distracting to you and the candidate.
- Allow the candidate time to ask questions. This is where you can elaborate on the Organization, your lab, and/or the specific job.
- Inform the candidate about maxi flex, leave, benefits, holidays, etc.

Some suggested interview questions can be found in TIPS ON INTERVIEWING.

Closing

If the candidate won't be considered further, close the interview diplomatically. If you are interested in the candidate, you may:

- Ask if the candidate is still interested in the position.
- Inform the candidate of the next step. Be prepared to advice on the timeframe for selection and how the selectee will be notified.

- Inform the candidate that references will be checked.
- Thank the candidate for coming for the interview, applying for the position, and/or having an interest in the Organization and position.
- Write up your notes.

Follow Up

A good customer service practice is to write all candidates acknowledging the interview and thanking the person for showing an interest in the organization. You may wish to do so after a selection has been made.

TIPS ON INTERVIEWING

Questions/ Assessment Tools

Careful thought should be given to constructing the interview.

Together with the KSAs (knowledge, skills, and abilities) and SPFs (selective placement factors) you used in the vacancy announcement, the kind of questions you ask will determine the type of person you select for your position. There are various assessment tools available to evaluate candidates including:

A.   The Behavioral Event Inventory (BEI). The candidate describes, in detail, a past experience that demonstrates the KSA or competency to a panel. The panel is facilitated by a person trained in the method. The phases of the process include planning, orientation, and interviewing, debriefing, and follow-up documentation.

B.   The Traditional Interview. Questions are developed prior to the interview. The same basic questions are asked of each candidate. Additionally the interviewer can,
   *   Encourage the candidate to give an example of a real situation, activity, or problem that includes: a description of the context, or environment; evidence or characteristics of the audience; the action taken; and the outcome.
   *   Ask open-ended questions. Asking yes and no questions will severely limit the kind of information you obtain from the interview. The only yes or no question you should ask is, "Are you still interested in this position?"

Interview Questions To Get You Started

   *   What interests you most about our position?
   *   What role do you take in a group situation? Give an example.
   *   Why do you want to work for our organization?
   *   What are your short-term and long-term goals?
   *   What are the two biggest accomplishments in your life?
   *   What has been your greatest technical achievement in your current position? Your career?
   *   Describe your participation in professional associations.
   *   What planning processes have you found useful? In what way do you feel you have improved in your planning abilities/methods?

- How does your past experience impact your qualifications for this position?

Supervisor and Manager Competencies

When preparing for supervisory or managerial interviews (whether using traditional or BEI), all candidates must be evaluated using the following two competencies:

A. Leading People. This competency includes conflict management, cultural awareness, team building, mentoring, and integrity/honesty (either work related or outside experience). Ask each candidate to describe a situation, problem, or event that demonstrates:
- Ability to work with a diverse group.
- Ability to prevent or mediate a conflict or disagreement or overcome dissension in a group.
- Ability to instill trust and confidence in others.
- Use of skills and abilities as a leader under stressful conditions.

B. Building Coalitions/Communications. This competency includes oral and/or written communication, influencing/negotiating, partnering, interpersonal skills, and political savvy. Ask each candidate to describe a situation, problem or event that demonstrates:

- Ability to express ideas or give instructions not easily or readily understood by their audience.
- Ability to make presentations to groups in order to gain acceptance of an idea by the group.
- Negotiating skills to gain approval for change or modification to programs, procedures, etc.

Interviewing People With Disabilities

Concentrate on the applicant's technical and professional knowledge, skills, abilities, experiences and interests, not on the disability. Remember, you cannot interview a disability, hire a disability or supervise a disability. You can interview a person, hire a person, and supervise a person.

The American with Disabilities Act (ADA) separates the hiring process into three stages: pre-offer, post-offer and employment. At each stage, the rules differ regarding the permissibility of disability-related questions and medical examinations. Definition of a "Disability-Related Question" means a question that is likely to elicit information about the disability. Definition of "Medical Examination" is a procedure or test that seeks information about an individual's physical or mental impairments or health.

Therefore, the two most important questions for employers to address are:

- Is the question disability-related or is the examination medical? And
- Where are we (i.e., at which stage - pre-offer, post-offer, or employment) in the employment process?

At the first stage (the pre-offer stage), the ADA prohibits all disability-related questions and medical examinations, even if the questions or examinations are related to the job. At the second stage (after the applicant is given a conditional job offer), the law allows all disability-related questions and medical examinations, as long as all entering employees in the job category are asked the questions or given the examinations. At the third stage (after the employee starts work), the law permits disability-related questions and medical examinations only if they are job-related and consistent with business necessity.

The law requires that medical information collected at any stage must be kept confidential.

For examples of some commonly asked questions on "Pre-employment Disability - Related Questions and Medical Examination Questions," please refer to the Equal Employment Opportunity Commission website at www.eeoc.gov/docs/preempl.

Accommodating Persons With Disabilities For An Interview

- Application and interviewing procedures should comply with the American with Disabilities Act (ADA). The ADA prohibits disability-related questions or medical exams before a real job offer is made.
- Agencies employment offices and interviewing location(s) are to be accessible to applicants with mobility, visual, hearing or cognitive disabilities.
- Be willing to make appropriate and reasonable accommodations to enable a job applicant with a disability to present him or herself in the best possible light. When setting up the interview explain what the

hiring process involves and ask the individual if he or she will need reasonable accommodations for any part of the interview process. For example, if a person who is blind states he or she will need help filling out forms, provide the assistance; provide an interpreter for an applicant who is deaf, if he or she requests one; provide details or specific instructions to applicants with cognitive disabilities, if this type of accommodation is required.

- Do not let a rehabilitation counselor, social worker or other third party take an active part in or sit in on an interview unless the applicant requests it.
- Make sure that all questions asked during the interview are job-related. Speak to essential job functions regarding the position for which the applicant is applying, as well as why, how, where, when and by whom each task or operation is performed. Do not ask whether or not the individual needs an accommodation to perform these functions, because such information is likely to reveal whether or not the individual has a disability. This is an ADA requirement to ensure that an applicant with a disability in not excluded before a real job offer is made.

Interview Do's and Don'ts

DO...

- Be friendly to establish rapport, help the candidate feel at ease.
- Listen attentively.
- Keep the interview under control. If the interviewee becomes verbose or drifts off the subject, it's your job to get back on track.
- Use professional terminology to evaluate the candidate's knowledge.
- Consider potential as well as current ability.
- Note the kinds of questions the candidate asks. Do they concern opportunities for self-improvement and increased responsibilities, or only pay and fringe benefits?
- Be objective.   Know yourself and your stereotypes.
- Understand that we tend to hire people who look like us.
- Be honest, even if it means saying something negative (e.g., the facility is old and there is not much office space). Just don't overemphasize it.
- Observe the candidate.
- Relax and enjoy the interview.

DON'T...

- Talk too much.
- Use a rigid or overly standardized approach. If you've prepared your questions, you can be flexible during the interview, knowing that you can easily get back on track. You'll become more flexible and react easily to different situations and personalities as you gain experience.
- Try to impress the interviewee with your knowledge.
- Hide demands of the job. A good candidate reacts favorably to these.
- Make commitments you may regret or are not authorized to make.
- Be satisfied with surface facts. Look for reasons, and probe.
- Take detailed notes. It may keep you from observing nonverbal responses and maintaining the conversational flow.
- Ask questions in a way that indicates the answers you want.
- Ask convoluted or over-defined questions.
- Be aggressive or evasive.
- Raise candidates' hopes when they are not likely to be selected.

CHECKING REFERENCES

You have completed the interviews, but you are not done yet.

A resume and interview are great tools, but the reference check is really the only way you have to verify information given by the candidates.

Normally, you will conduct a reference check on the one or two finalists. Reliability of the reference check is based on the concept that past performance is a good predictor of future performance. Reference checks will help:

- Verify information the candidate provided both in the application and during the interview.
- You gain insight into who your candidates are and how they behave in the workplace.

Never make an offer (remember, you can only make a tentative offer) without first doing an exhaustive check of the candidate's background. A comprehensive reference check goes back 5 years and includes contacting a minimum of three sources that are knowledgeable about the candidate's abilities. Contact

Enough references to confirm the quality of your selection.

Which References Should I Check?

- Academic references—institutions and teachers/professors.
- Current and former supervisors—immediate supervisors are often the best sources for reliable information about a candidate's work performance.
- Your network of professional associates/associations.
- Candidate's personal references—they will generally provide a favorable reference. Ask them for names and positions of other persons who know the candidate and contact them.
- Candidate's colleagues—business or work associates will sometimes provide an objective analysis of the candidate's strengths and weaknesses.
- Seek your own independent sources who know the candidate.

Tips for Checking References

- Ask only job-related questions and ask the same questions about each candidate.
- Ask open-ended questions and probe.
- Use telephone reference checks rather than mail inquiries since they are faster and less time consuming.
- Keep the conversation casual. If you speak to the person in a relaxed manner, you will get better results.
- If the reference provider keeps talking, keep listening and asking more questions. Seek out judgmental comments and try to read between the lines of what the person is telling you. A reference who says the candidate tried hard or is a people person may be saying such things to avoid talking about real problems or issues.
- Do not eliminate one candidate because of poor references and then neglect to check references from the remaining candidate(s).
- Always check dates and times the person giving the reference worked with or supervised the candidate, and then
- Determine if there is a personal relationship.
- Give only a general description of the vacant position. Too many details may bias the reference person in formulating their answers. As in the case of the employment interview, let the other person do most of the talking.
- Do not use leading questions such as "He's a good manager, isn't he?"
- Do not let a prominent characteristic, such as a good academic record; overshadow less obvious or possibly negative traits, such as a poor leave record.
- Speak to someone in addition to the current supervisor. A dishonest supervisor may try to unload a problem employee by giving a glowing reference.
- Listen carefully to the answers you are given and take notes.

The Reference Check Questions To Ask

When contacting a reference, we recommend you begin with,

"Thank you for taking a few moments to provide information about our job candidate. The information you provide will be considered along with other information submitted by the applicant and other references. Please be aware that under the Federal government's employment policies, we may become obligated to disclose the information to the applicant or others involved in the selection or review process."

Then, ask and record the answers to the following:

- How long have you known the candidate?
- In what capacity were you associated with the candidate? As employer? Supervisor? Co-worker? Friend? Other?
- Using a scale of 1-5, with 1 being poor and 5 being excellent, how would you rate the candidate in comparison to most others you have known.

	RATINGS 1 2 3 4 5
Work ethic?	_____
Work quality?	_____
Technical skills?	_____
Writing skills?	_____
Communication skills?	_____
Interpersonal skills?	_____
Reliability & dependability?	_____
Receptivity to feedback?	_____
Adaptability to change?	_____
Ability to deal with job stress?	_____

- What would you consider to be some of this candidate's most positive attributes or strengths?
- What would you consider to be some areas where this person is not as strong or needs to improve?
- What type of work environment does the candidate require to excel?
- Describe the candidate's initiative, personality, and negative habits.
- How does the candidate get along with customers? Co-workers? Supervisors and managers?
- Is the candidate reliable? Honest? Trustworthy? Of good character?
- Would you rehire the candidate?
- Is there any other information concerning the candidate's qualifications, character, conduct and general fitness I should know about?

Prohibited Questions and Practices

- Please do not put yourself in a position of engaging in a prohibited personnel practice related to employment and selection. As a selecting official with the authority to take, direct others to take, recommend, or approve any personnel action, you must not:

- Discriminate for or against any employee or candidate for employment on the basis of race, color, national origin, gender, religion, age, disability, political beliefs, sexual orientation, and marital or family status.
- Deceive or willfully obstruct any person with respect to such person's right to compete for employment.
- Influence any person to withdraw from competition for any position for the purpose of improving or injuring the prospects of any other person for employment.
- Appoint or employ a relative to a position over which you exercise jurisdiction or control as a selecting official.
- Take or fail to take a personnel action with respect to a candidate for employment as a reprisal.
- Discriminate for or against a candidate for employment on the basis of conduct which does not adversely affect the performance of the candidate or the performance of others (except for criminal behavior).

RECORDING A PROFILE OF IMPRESSIONS

Candidate's Name_____

1. What are the candidate's strongest assets in relation to the requirements for this position?

2. What are the candidate's shortcomings in relation to this position?

3. The candidate seemed knowledgeable about/ interested in:

4. Contradictions or inconsistencies noted were:

5. The candidate was evasive about:

6. Overall, the candidate responded to questions with: (e.g., openness, confidence, poise, directness, glibness, evasiveness, etc.) Examples?

7. Overall, reference checks were positive, mediocre, less than positive. Examples/key descriptions or characteristics?

Supervisory and Managerial Competencies:

Leading People is there evidence demonstrating:

1. Ability to gain commitment and support from others?

2. Ability to develop solutions to management problems?

3. Ability to establish performance objectives?

4. Ability to foster cooperative working environment among employees?

5. Ability to deal with morale and employee concerns?

Building Coalitions/Communication:

Is there evidence demonstrating:

1. Conflict resolution?

2. Working as a member of a team?

3. Expression of ideas and views that others understand and that influence (persuade) them to act?

RECRUITING CINEMATOGRAPHERS - IT TAKES MORE THAN A JOB ANNOUNCEMENT

Job searcher - here is the recruiter's perspective on the placement process, written from the perspective of the recruiter, the full inside scoop, to enable you to know what is going on begind the scenes and prepare for it.

One of the critical steps in the recruitment process involves the actions you take to speed up the process and reach the largest, desirable pool of candidates.

Simply posting the vacancy on job websites will not guarantee that you receive quality applications for the job. This chapter provides suggestions on steps YOU should take to ensure YOUR recruitment activity works for YOU.

Considering these suggestions can help minimize the time required for recruitment on YOUR end and also help the Human Resources (HR) Specialist speed up the process.

Before Submitting the Vacancy

Review and rethink the position description
- Ensure that the duties and responsibilities reflect the needs (or discipline) of the position at this time.
- Determine if it accurately reflects the knowledge, skills, and abilities (KSAs) needed to perform the job.
- Ensure that the KSAs can be directly related back to duties and responsibilities in the position description.
- Develop your "Quality Experience" definition. Identify experience a candidate will need to bring to the job on day one.

Consider alternative hiring methods
- Determine if the position can be filled using the Student Career Experience Program (SCEP), Federal Career Intern Program, Career Enhancement Program, and USDA Direct Hire Authority, special hiring authorities for individuals with disabilities or veterans, or other hiring methods.

Think about the vacancy announcement

- Determine who the applicants are you are trying to reach.
- Determine if you will need to recruit nationwide or if there will be sufficient candidates in the local commuting area to give you a diverse applicant pool from which to select.

Develop a strategy to reach your candidate
- Identify ways to market the job announcement to reach potential applicants.
- Visit or contact the Career Center, Deans, and Professors if you are located on a campus to promote and highlight the many career opportunities available with ARS.
- Identify colleagues (both within and outside the organization) who can help in marketing the job.
- Identify colleges and universities or professional societies and organizations where the announcement should be mailed.
- Identify newspapers, journals, or online advertising sites that might be useful in marketing the job.
- Contact the Recruitment Office and your Area Civil Rights Manager for ideas on how to reach a diverse candidate pool.

Contact your servicing HR Specialist
- Discuss recruitment strategies and alternatives, as well as expectations for completion of the action.
- Keep in touch with your HR Specialist by e-mail during the recruitment process.

Submit all required paperwork
- Submit all position descriptions and forms needed to request the personnel action.
- Submit draft ad text along with the request to save time (remember, your servicing HR Specialist must review and approve all ads prior to being placed).
- Submit your "Quality Experience" definition.

When the Vacancy Announcement is Open

Conduct your Marketing
- Be PROACTIVE!
- Personally identify potential candidates and send a note with the announcement or call to encourage them to apply – be cautious, however, and don't give the impression they will get the job.
- Send the vacancy announcement to individuals, schools and colleges, or organizations you have identified, and place ads in newspapers,

magazines, and online job boards.
- E-mail the announcement to co-workers, colleagues, stakeholders, and peers with a brief note asking for assistance in publicizing the job.
- Document your efforts.

Identify a Diverse Group of Interview Panel Members and Set Up Panel Dates
- Ask your HR Specialist for an approximate timeframe for receipt of the certificate of eligibles.
- Ask interview panel members to block out time on their calendars for the interview process.
- Clear your calendar also!
- Keep your interview panel members informed throughout the recruitment process – if conflicts arise, replace panel members immediately.

Develop Interview Questions
- Share interview questions with the panel members for comments and suggestions.

Contact Your HR Specialist Throughout The Process
- Ask if you are receiving applications.
- Determine if you need to extend the closing date. Ask your HR Specialist to scan applications received to get an idea of the quality of applicants before making a decision to extend the closing date.

Once the Certificate of Eligibles is Received

Schedule the Interviews Immediately So The Best Candidates Are Still Available
- Review the certificate right away and identify the candidates you believe should be interviewed. Ask for help from colleagues as needed. Set a timeframe to complete the interviews.
- Schedule the interviews close together to minimize losing a desirable candidate and to maximize the likelihood of remembering individual candidates' strengths and weaknesses.
- Have an open mind – interview "Preference Eligible" (Veterans and Displaced) candidates before making judgments on their ability to do the job. Remember, if they are on the certificate, they meet the qualifications for the position. Talk to your HR Specialist if you have concerns.
- Advise applicants of your timeframe for conducting the interviews – if they are interested, they will make themselves available.

- Advise the candidates of the process you will use to conduct interviews (for example, interview panel – give them guidelines).

Conduct Reference Check
- Always conduct reference checks on top candidates! This is more critical than ever before.

Make Your Tentative Selection
- Contact the candidate selected to advise that their name is being recommended to Human Resources. Ask if any issues with pay, incentives, EOD, etc.
- Notify HR Specialist of your decision and discuss options for offering recruitment incentives. Remember, the HR Specialist must make the official offer of employment.
- Obtain required area/organization approvals of the selection and incentives being proposed.
- Ask the HR Specialist to issue the written employment offer including information on negotiated pay, recruitment incentives and bonuses, and EOD date.

After The Selection is Made

Notify other candidates interviewed of your decision
- HR will notify all non-selected candidates of the final outcome.
- Contact the candidates interviewed and encourage them to apply for other positions.

Share impressive applications
- Share other impressive applications with colleagues who may be recruiting for similar jobs – they can contact and encourage quality applicants to apply for their positions.
- Share a copy of other impressive applications with the Recruitment Office – this office can refer the applications to others recruiting for similar positions.

Prepare for the new employee/s arrival
- Make copies of appropriate policies, procedures, and other documents the new employee should read.
- Have the employee's workspace cleaned up and the desk stocked with essential supplies.
- Prepare the performance plan and provide it along with a copy of the position description on the first day of work.

- Set time on your calendar to spend with the new employee on the first day – show them around the facility, discuss the job and work they will be doing, provide time to read through materials, and let the employee know they can ask questions.
- Make sure the employee is set up with an e-mail address and computer access, etc.
- Identify a mentor and develop an Individual Development Plan (IDP) to address with the employee.
- Inform the employee of the probationary period requirements as well as the promotion potential, if any, of the position.

ASSESSING YOUR RECRUITMENT AND SELECTION PRACTICES

Policies and Procedures

This completes your view from the other side of the table, the recruiters' - and helps you in understanding their workload and point of view.

Your organization's policies and procedures should thoroughly document the recruitment, assessment and selection processes.

The policies and procedures should be accessible and understood by not only HR professionals but Managers and others involved in the hiring process.

Ask yourself these questions to help assess whether or not your organization's policies and procedures are current and include new requirements.

- Are recruitment, assessment and selection processes supported by written policies and procedures that are up-to-date, accurate and complete? (Ideally within 2 years.)
- How widely communicated are the organization's written recruitment, assessment and selection policies to those who are involved in the process? (Ideally to all staff.)
- Does the organization utilize these policies and procedures for the recruitment, assessment and selection processes?
- Does the organization have a written policy describing procedures for the review of competencies and/or qualifications?
- Does the organization follow a formal recruitment, assessment and selection plan at the start of each recruitment? (Link to sample recruitment plan)
- Training Managers, supervisors, and personnel involved in the hiring process should receive comprehensive training in the organization's full recruitment process and thoroughly understand proper interview and selection techniques.
- Who performs recruitment activities for the organization? (Ideally HR with unit management participation.)
- On average, how long does it take to fill a position within the organization from the start of recruitment until an offer is extended? (Ideally 2 months or less.)
- Does the organization provide training and/or written guidelines about

recruitment, assessment and selection policies and procedures to managers and supervisors prior to them seeking to fill a position (e.g., reviewing applications, conducting interviews, and evaluating candidates)?

Recruitment Strategies

The organization should tailor their recruitment strategy to meet the need for the specific position and the organization's goals, as well as attract a diverse pool of applicants.
* Does the organization develop a specific recruiting and marketing plan to identify how and who they need to contact to help achieve finding the best candidates?
* Does the organization have a plan to recruit qualified applicants who represent the diversity of the State or local service area?
* Does the organization compare its workforce demographics to the State, county or local labor force demographics?
* Does the organization utilize specialized recruitment strategies to attract hard-to-find, qualified candidates?
* What recruitment strategies are utilized to attract hard-to-find qualified candidates? (Ideally executive search firms, internet job sites, local and regional newspapers, job fairs, professional organizations, civic organizations, networking, Employment Security Department, etc.)
* Does the organization track the effectiveness of different recruiting methods?
* Are recruitment sources periodically evaluated to assure they meet the needs of the organization and return on investment calculated?

Recruitment Process and Hiring
* Recruitment procedures should be developed and administered in compliance with all applicable organization policies, bargaining agreements, laws, regulations, and professional standards.
* Is a job analysis conducted to identify the key responsibilities of a position prior to announcement?
* Are required qualifications reviewed prior to position announcements to assure they are job related?
* Are preferred qualifications reviewed prior to position announcements to assure they are job related?
* Does the organization's HR staff assure all applicants selected for employment meet the posted qualifications for the position?
* What percentage of job announcements identify the competencies needed to perform the job?

- Are essential functions of the position discussed with the candidate?
- Does the organization utilize a behavioral interviewing tool to develop standardized, relevant interview questions?

Selection Process
- Selection procedures should be developed and administered in compliance with all applicable laws, regulations, and professional standards.
- What methods are used for the selection process? (Ideally selection matrix, interview notes, resume ranking, skills testing, reference checks, background checks, etc.)
- What percentage of the final selection decisions is documented? (This includes reasons for hire versus non-hire.)
- How long is the selection documentation retained?
- Does the organization evaluate and assess how well the selection procedures worked?
- How frequently does the organization assess its selection procedures?
- Does the organization maintain documentation of the assessment process?

Glossary

A

Annual: recurring, done, or performed every year; yearly

Applicant: a person who formally applies for a job

Apprenticeship: a formal relationship between the worker and sponsor that consists of a combination of on-the-job training and related occupation-specific instruction. Apprenticeship programs usually provide at least 144 hours of occupation-specific technical instruction and 2,000 hours of on-the-job training per year over a 3- to 5-year period. Apprenticeships are associated mostly with the trades. Examples of occupations that utilize apprenticeships are electricians and structural iron and steel workers; see On-the-job training

Associate's degree: degree awarded usually for at least 2 years of full-time academic study beyond high school; see Education

Average: the quantity calculated by adding a set of numbers and dividing the resulting sum by the quantity of numbers summed; see Mean

B

Bachelor's degree: degree awarded usually for at least 4 years of full-time academic study beyond high school; see Education

Base year: year used as a reference point for comparison with later years. For example, 2010 is the base year for the 2010–2020 employment projections. Employment in the base year is actual 2010 data, whereas employment in the target, or projection, year is projected

Business cycle: The periods of growth and decline in an economy. There are four stages in the cycle: expansion, when the economy grows; peak, the high point of an expansion; contraction, when the economy slows down; and trough, the low point of a contraction

Baby-boom generation: individuals born between 1946 and 1964

C

Certification: award for demonstrating competency in a skill or set of skills, typically through the passage of an examination, work experience, training, or some combination thereof. Certification is always voluntary. Some certification programs may require a certain level of educational achievement for eligibility.

Consolidation: the merger of two or more commercial interests or corporations

Current Population Survey (CPS): a national survey that samples 60,000 households on a monthly basis and collects information on labor force characteristics of the U.S. civilian noninstitutional population; the CPS is conducted by the Census Bureau for the Bureau of Labor Statistics

D
Demand for workers: total job openings resulting from employment growth and the need to replace workers who leave jobs

Doctoral or professional degree: degree awarded usually for at least 3 years of full-time academic work beyond a bachelor's degree; for example, some science and other occupations need a doctoral degree, and all lawyers, physicians, and dentists need a professional degree for employment; see Education

Domestic sourcing: moving jobs to lower cost regions of the United States instead of to other countries

Duties: the major tasks or activities that employees in an occupation usually perform

E
Earnings: Pay or wages of a worker or group of workers for services performed during a specific period—for example, hourly, daily, weekly, or annually. Also see Pay, Wages

Education: levels of education typically needed for entry into an occupation are classified as follows:

Doctoral or professional degree: degree awarded usually for at least 3 years of full-time academic work beyond a bachelor's degree; e.g., lawyers, physicians and surgeons, and dentists

Master's degree: degree awarded usually for 1 or 2 years of full-time academic study beyond a bachelor's degree

Bachelor's degree: degree awarded usually for at least 4 years of full-time academic study beyond high school

Associate's degree: degree awarded usually for at least 2 years of full-time academic study beyond high school

Postsecondary nondegree award: usually a certificate or other award that is not a degree. Certifications issued by professional organizations or certifying bodies are not included in this category. Programs may last only a few weeks to 2 years. e.g., nursing aides, EMTs and paramedics, and hairstylists

Some college, no degree: a high school diploma or the equivalent, plus the completion of one or more postsecondary courses that did not result in any degree or award

High school diploma or equivalent: the completion of high school or the equivalent resulting in the award of a high school diploma or the equivalent, such as the General Education Development (GED) credential

Less than high school: the completion of any level of primary or secondary education that did not result in the awarding of a high school diploma or the equivalent

Employment growth/shrinkage: increase or decrease in the number of jobs

Entry level: the starting level for workers who are new to an occupation; different occupations may require different levels of education, training, or experience upon entry

Employed: the situation of a person who has an agreement with an employer to work full time, part time, or on a contractual basis for that employer

Employment: the number of jobs in an occupation, including full-time, part-time, and self-employed. For example, employment of accountants and auditors was 1,216,900 in 2010

F

Fieldwork: an investigation or search for material, data, etc., made in the field as opposed to the classroom, the laboratory, or official headquarters. For example, archeologists working at a dig site in the desert; historians or curators finding or collecting artifacts for museums; and environmental technicians collecting water samples from a pond, a stream, or an ocean

Fixed work schedules: schedules of employees who work the same hours on an ongoing basis—for example, 9 a.m.–5p.m.; see Work schedules

Flexible work schedules: schedules of employees who set their own hours within specified guidelines and with a fixed number of total hours; see Work schedules

Full time: 35 hours or more per week, according to the Current Population Survey; see Work schedules

G

GDP (gross domestic product): the market value of all final goods and services produced within a country in a given period; the most commonly used measure of the size of the overall economy. The Bureau of Economic Analysis (BEA) produces estimates of GDP.

GED (General Educational Development): a credential signifying the completion of a program that is equivalent to a high school curriculum; see Education

Greater than full time: more than 40 hours per week; see Work schedules

Growth rate: the percent change in the number of jobs added or lost in a U.S. occupation or industry over a given projection period; see "Information Found in the Occupational Outlook Handbook"; growth rate adjectives used in the OOH are defined by the following percent changes for the 2010–20 employment projections:

much faster than the average: 29 percent or more
faster than the average: 20 percent to 28 percent
as fast as the average: 10 percent to 19 percent
more slowly than the average: 3 percent to 9 percent
little or no change: –2 percent to 2 percent

decline moderately: −3 percent to −9 percent
decline rapidly: −10 percent or less
H
High school diploma or equivalent: award or credential that is equivalent to a high school diploma, such as a high school diploma itself or the General Educational Development (GED) credential; see Education

Household: all persons who occupy a housing unit

I
Important qualities: characteristics and personality traits that are likely needed for workers to be successful in given occupations

Industry: a group of establishments that produce similar products or provide similar services; see NAICS

Internship: training under supervision in a professional setting. This category does not include internships that are suggested for advancement; see On-the-job training

Injury and illness rate: ratio expressing the number of workers sustaining a wound, strain, or infection due to an incident or exposure at the workplace per 100 workers; the Occupational Safety and Health Administration (OSHA) considers an injury or illness to be work related if an event or exposure in the work environment either caused or contributed to the resulting condition or significantly aggravated a preexisting condition; in general, a Handbook profile will cite an injury and illness rate only if it is particularly high compared with the rate for all other occupations

J
Job openings: job openings occur when occupations grow, creating new jobs, and when workers leave an occupation permanently, resulting in the need to replace them

Job: a specific instance of employment; a position of employment to be filled at an establishment; see Employment

Job outlook: a statement that conveys the projected rate of growth or decline in employment in an occupation over the next 10 years; also compares the projected growth rate with that projected for all other occupations; Also see growth rate

Job prospects: a qualitative measure of the competition for jobs that takes into consideration factors such as the growth or decline in numbers of jobs, the expected number of qualified workers, and/or the expected number of applicants; a comparison of the number of jobs with the number of potential workers and jobseekers

K
No entries

L
Labor force: the sum of all persons 16 years and older in the civilian noninstitutional population who are either employed, or unemployed but available for work and actively looking for work

Less than high school: the completion of any level of primary or secondary education that did not result in the awarding of a high school diploma or the equivalent; see Education

Less than 1 year (of work experience in a related occupation): the level of experience in another occupation typically needed for entry into a given occupation; see Required training for entry; also Work experience in a related occupation

Long-term on-the-job training: more than 12 months of on-the-job training or programs not including apprenticeships; see On-the-job training

Licenses: permission granted by government agencies or other accrediting bodies that allows for the selling of certain goods or services

M
Master's degree: degree awarded usually for 1 or 2 years of full-time academic study beyond a bachelor's degree; see Education

Mean: the mathematical average of a set of numbers, calculated by adding the numbers and dividing the total by the number of numbers summed; see Average

Median: the middle number in an ordered list of numbers

Moderate-term on-the-job training: 1 to 12 months of on-the-job training or programs, not including apprenticeships; see On-the-job training

More than 5 years (of work experience in a related occupation): the number of years of experience in a related occupation typically needed for entry into a given occupation; see Required training for entry; also Work experience in a related occupation

N
North American Industry Classification System (NAICS): Industry classification system used by federal statistical agencies in classifying business establishments for the purpose of collecting, analyzing, and publishing statistical data related to the U.S. economy

New job: an addition of a position to an establishment's payroll, usually as a result of economic expansion

Nonfixed work schedules: schedules of employees who work different hours on one job; often used to accommodate particular traits of individual workers or because the work required by the employers varies for each individual; see Work schedules

None (on-the-job training): the situation when no additional occupation-specific training or preparation is typically required to attain competency in an occupation; see On-the-job training

None (required training for entry): the situation when no work experience in a related occupation is typically required to enter a given occupation; see Required training for entry; also Work experience in a related occupation

Number of jobs: number of actual instances of employment according to the BLS National Employment Matrix; see the projection methods page for more information about the Matrix

Numeric change in employment: a projected change in the number of jobs in an occupation or industry

O

On-the-job training: training or preparation that is typically needed, once employed in an occupation, to attain competency in the occupation. Training is occupation specific rather than job specific; skills learned can be transferred to another job in the same occupation

Internship/Residency: training under supervision in a professional setting. This category does not include internships that are suggested for advancement.

Apprenticeship: a formal relationship between a worker and his or her sponsor that consists of a combination of on-the-job training and related occupation-specific instruction. Apprenticeship programs usually provide at least 144 hours of occupation-specific technical instruction and 2,000 hours of on-the-job training per year over a 3-to-5-year period. Apprenticeships are associated mostly with the trades. Examples of occupations that utilize apprenticeships include electricians and structural iron and steel workers.

Long-term on-the-job training: more than 12 months of on-the-job training or programs, not including apprenticeships.

Moderate-term on-the-job training: 1 to 12 months of combined on-the-job experience and informal training

Short-term on-the-job training: 1 month or less of combined on-the-job experience and informal training

None: no additional occupation-specific training or preparation

Occupation: a craft, trade, profession, or other means of earning a living. Also, a set of activities or tasks that employees are paid to perform and that together go by a certain name. Employees who are in the same occupation perform essentially the same tasks, whether or not they work in the same industry

P

Pay: Earnings or wages of a worker or a group of workers for services performed during a specific period—for example, hourly, daily, weekly, or annually. Also see Earnings, Wages

Part time: less than 35 hours of work per week, according to the Current Population Survey; see Work schedules

Percent: one part in a hundred. For example, 62 percent (also written 62%) means 62 parts out of 100

Percentile wage estimate: the value of a wage below which a certain percentage of workers fall

Percent change in employment: growth rates expressed as percentages

Personal consumption: total goods and services purchased by individuals in the U.S. economy; the amount of goods and services used or purchased by individuals or households in the U.S. economy; a key statistic in measuring or calculating overall GDP

Population: The total number of inhabitants of the United States

Postsecondary nondegree award: a certificate or other credential that is awarded by an educational institution upon completion of formal postsecondary schooling. (The postsecondary nondegree certificate is different from certifications issued by professional organizations or certifying bodies.) Postsecondary nondegree award programs may last from just a few weeks to 2 years. Examples of those who need postsecondary nondegree awards are nursing aides, emergency medical technicians, and hairstylists ; see Education

Q
Qualifications: personality traits, education, training, work experience, or other qualities workers need to enter an occupation

Important qualities: characteristics and personality traits that are likely needed for workers to be successful in given occupations

R
Related occupations: occupations that have similar job duties; see Similar occupations

Replacement rate: the rate at which workers permanently leave the occupations in which they are employed; large occupations that have high replacement rates need many workers to fill jobs that are vacated.

Replacement needs: the number of projected openings expected to result from workers who retire or permanently leave an occupation; replacement needs are calculated from monthly CPS data

Residency: training under supervision in a professional setting. This category does not include internships that are suggested for advancement; see On-the-job training

Rotating work schedules: schedules that have a fixed number of hours and time off over a period of more than 1 week, but not a set weekly schedule, according to data from the 2010 Current Population Survey; see Work schedules

S
Salary: earnings of a worker or a group of workers for services performed during a specific period—for example, an hourly straight-time wage rate or, for workers not paid on an hourly basis, straight-time earnings divided by hours worked

Seasonal employment: employment that is not expected to last a full year, but that may reoccur; for example, many retail sales associates are hired only for the busy holiday season, and forest firefighters are more likely to be employed during the summer months, when vegetation is dryer

Short-term on-the-job training: 1 month or less of on-the-job experience and informal training; see On-the-job training

Similar occupations: occupations that tend to share common daily tasks or require similar skill sets, rather than similar wages or education

Self-employed: those who work for profit or fees in their own business, profession, trade, or farm; only the unincorporated self-employed are included in the self-employed category

SOC code: the Standard Occupational Classification (SOC) system, which is used by all federal statistical agencies to classify workers into occupational categories for the purpose of collecting, calculating, or disseminating data

Some college, no degree: a high school diploma or equivalent, plus the completion of one or more postsecondary courses that did not result in a degree or award; see Education

Supply of workers: the number of people in the labor force; for most occupations, the supply of workers is smaller than the total number in the labor force because the supply is limited to those with particular education or training requirements

T
Training: see On-the-job training; or Required training for entry; or Work experience in a related occupation

U
Undergraduate degree: Bachelor's degree; see Education

Union membership: the group of workers who join labor unions, hold union memberships, and enjoy benefits of the organized, coordinated efforts of the union to improve the work environment

V
Vocational school: a secondary school that teaches vocational trades, such as construction trades; vocational schools may or may not award degrees; see Education

W
Wage: earnings or pay of a worker or a group of workers for services performed during a specific period—for example, hourly, daily, weekly, or annually. Also see Earnings, Pay

Work schedules: the number of daily hours, weekly hours, and annual weeks that employees in an occupation are scheduled to, and do, work. Short-term fluctuations and one-time events are not considered unless the change becomes permanent; for more details, visit Work Schedules in the National Compensation Survey

Fixed work schedules: schedules under which employees who work those schedules do so on an ongoing basis; e.g., 9 a.m.–5 p.m.

Flexible work schedules: schedules under which employees set their own hours within guidelines and with a fixed number of total hours

Rotating work schedules: schedules that have a fixed number of hours and time off over a period of more than 1 week, but not a set weekly schedule

Nonfixed work schedules: schedules of employees who work different hours on one job; often utilized to accommodate particular traits of individual workers or because the work required varies by individual

Greater than full time: more than 40 hours per week

Full time: between 35 and 40 hours of work per week

Part time: Less than 35 hours of work per week

Work experience in a related occupation: the level of work experience in an occupation related to a given occupation; may be a typical method of entry into the given occupation

X, Y, Z
No entries

2273839R00055

Printed in Germany
by Amazon Distribution
GmbH, Leipzig